Philip spends much of his time training the corgis

TRADE
MARK

First published in Great Britain
by Sphere Books Ltd 1986
27 Wright's Lane,
London W8 5SW

Designed by
The Bloomsbury Group

Set by Witwell Ltd

Printed and bound in
Great Britain by
Collins, Glasgow

ISBN 0 7221 5158 3

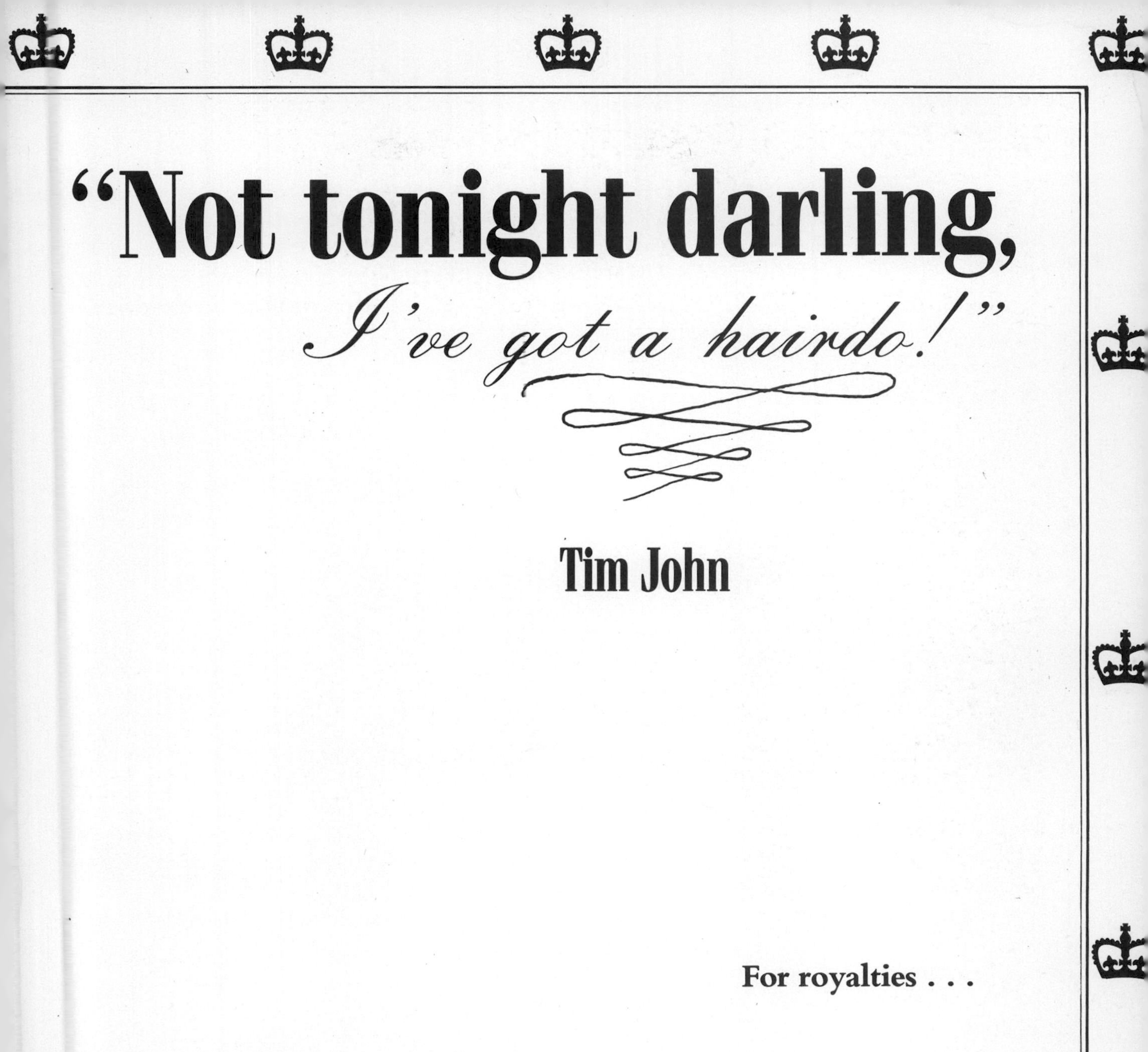

"Not tonight darling, *I've got a hairdo!*"

Tim John

For royalties . . .

SPHERE BOOKS LIMITED

PALLAS

POWER, PASSION & INTRIGUE WITH THE WORLD'S MOST-WATCHED FAMILY

Starring *"E.R."*. . . . . *"JOCK"*. . . . . . *& "VICTORIAN PRINCIPLES"* . . .

The story so far...

In history's longest-running soap opera, "E.R.", eldest child of "Miss Ellie", has descended from sixty-two previous bosses and now heads the family empire.
Just like the oil business, the royal business is run from the big family home. Complete with the father who's even more simplistic than Jock Ewing, three sons the old man regards as cowboys, a sister who's been through more booze than Sue Ellen, plus the couple who spend more time in the saddle than Ray and Donna.
In previous episodes E.R.'s sister has taken off with a pilot, married a photographer named after a Welsh mountain, had a few rakes in the garden and been through more fags than Rock Hudson.
An Austrian divorcee with a father in Hitler's SS has married into Pallas, but is suspected of having a lover in Dallas. A prince has hit the sack and the headlines with a porn queen, and all this for an annual production budget of a mere £6 million.
How can the other soaps compete?
But there's trouble ahead... A nursery teacher with no "O" levels has become an international cover-girl overnight and is set to overtake Pallas with the ultimate Sloane series...

AND COMING SOON!
WestEnders

The mega-million budget chart-topping soap in which the public fork out more on hairdos and dresses than Dallas and Dynasty put together!!!

If you think TV soap plots are unbelievable, just listen to some of these early PALLAS episodes, now available on video...

Tudor Holocaust

The family business is being run by a man with six wives. The first is his brother's widow. He gets fed up with her and secretly marries wife number two, who he promptly has bumped off for adultery. Wife three dies in child-birth. Wife four is divorced for being uglier than her portrait. Wife five is beheaded, so he marries number six, then dies from exhaustion and a nasty social disease. The business is taken over by his ten year old son followed by the boy's half-sister, the original 'E.R.'. 'E.R.' has a liking for ruff-trade, kills her cousin, walks over people's macs and sends the navy to burn off the King of Spain's beard!

Stuart Holocaust

If you enjoyed Rocky I, then Rocky II, don't miss Charles I followed by Charles II. Our story begins with Charles' old man, James, the notor-ious woofter and lunatic. Though his driving ambition is to show as many people as possible his bottom, James still manages to make bowling illegal on Sundays, write the first anti-smoking campaign and avoid an attempt to hold the first firework party in parliament. Then Charles takes over the business. There's a military coup and it's another good day for the axeman. Fearing the consequences, the next boss, Charles II hides up an oak tree. But the public don't want to miss another series of **PALLAS**, so Charles is reinstated. His wife gives him Bombay. He immediately duffs up the Dutch and thereby owns New York. Naturally he falls in love with an orange-seller.
Would you take all that from Cliff Barnes or Ken Barlow? Of course not. But **PALLAS** fans remain loyal followers. Even the contemporary **LOUIS QUATORZE, THE VERSAILLES YEARS** couldn't compete.

THE WINDSOR WAR

From the people who brought you Edward I, Edward II and all the other Edwards, now comes the sensational scandal, Edward VIII.

A Pennsylvanian girl has just divorced US Naval lieutenant coincidentally called Earl Spencer. She marries again. Divorces again and then meets PALLAS boss, Edward. PALLAS advisors warn him that it's just not on to bonk commoners. But Ed's crown over heels in love. A family feud begins, forcing the King to write his letter of resig-nation. The New York Journal ran the headline 'KING WILL WED WALLY', and the King runs away to France.

Meanwhile back down the Mall, they are preparing for war with the country they all came from. Arch baddie Edward gets tangled up in a secret Nazi plot to put him back on the throne. As punishment, he's given a massive house in the Bahamas and a hat with lots of feathers. From then on, it's a firm family rule that one should refrain from knocking up commoners or yanks. But they can't resist...

Filmed in Glorious Thronoscope!

Their Love Cost A Throne!

THE WINDSOR WAR

The THRONE RANGER Handbook

Far snottier than mere Sloane Rangers, true Thronies are the result of hundreds of years of interbreeding with upper-class krauts and chinless twits.

As if trained by Hooray Henry Higgins, their accents can crack champagne glasses at fifty paces. They generally have at least four christian names, and their etiquette is extraordinary . . . Only a true Throne Ranger would know exactly what to do when, in the middle of a garden party conversation with Her Majesty, a corgi attempts to mount their leg.

Needless to say, from the cream of the class crumpet to that dear old thronie "Superma'am", this double-barrelled brigade are all absolutely loaded. And they stash it away in Coutts — the bank that likes to say "*yar*".

"ITE"

- Crowns
- Venison roasts
- Royal appointments
- Carriages
- Hands held behind backs
- Balding crowns
- The Tatler
- Street cred
- Military bands
- Royal tours
- Royal jelly
- Opening parliament
- Rover 3500s
- Royal waves
- Christmas speeches

Throne Ranger roadsigns

Pleb's car up ahead

Speed limit 60-ish

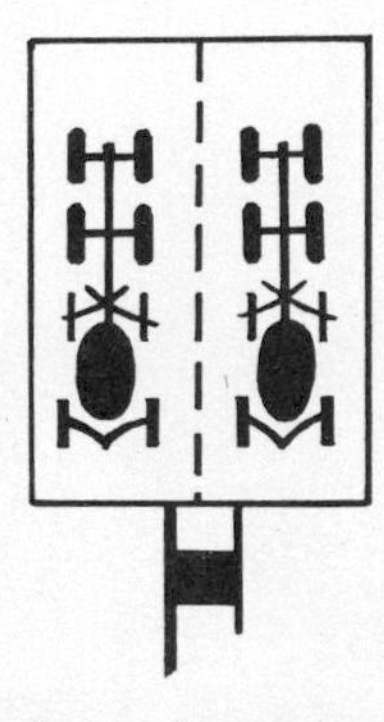
Dual carriageway

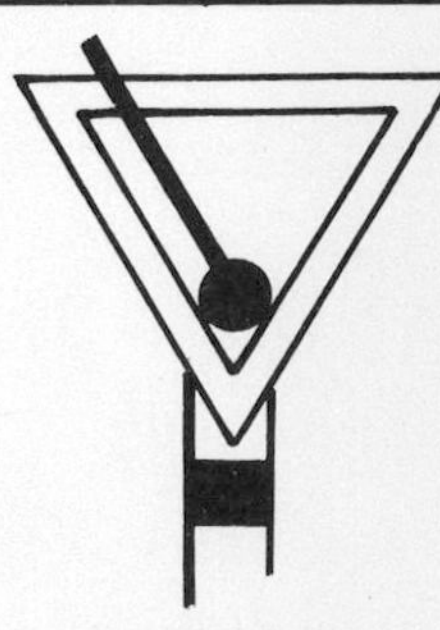
One of the few things Margaret gives way to

"IN"

- 3 million quid headbands
- Wholemeal baps and nut bakes
- Hair appointments
- Claridges
- One hand on hip, the other pointing straight up to the sky
- Heir restorers
- "The Prattler", the magazine for people who sound like Di
- Mall cred
- Personal stereo sets
- Royal gigs
- Royal spermbank sales
- Open-air pop concerts
- GTi-s or 325i-s
- Head tilting and giggling
- Christmas charity records

The Throne Ranger Christmas

Christmas begins with the Thronies opening the green wellies they hang on the ends of their beds in place of stockings. Inside this year's welly, Her Majesty received a musical loo roll holder that plays the National Anthem. This has all the other Thronies in hysterics because guests have to stand up when it plays.

Another little "Throne-room" pressie was the loo roll with photos of Margaret Thatcher on every sheet.

Other pressies included Willy's "*Tea Party Set*", with place settings for 400, Diana's new L.P. "*Wham! Bam! Thank-you, Ma'arm!*", "*Heir-raising*" by Sir Alistair Barnet, and for someone else, the new book, "*Adolf Hitler – My part in his family tree.*" Before chapel, there is the traditional placing of whoopee cushions on bishop's seats, followed by Liz's thank you for this year's presents, in particular the six million quid towards the house-keeping.

After dinner, the whole family plays charades. (They also play this every other day of the year). And throughout the Christmas period, Dad tries to stick Charles on top of the tree.

"Not tonight darling, I've got a hairdo!"

101 Uses for a dead corgi

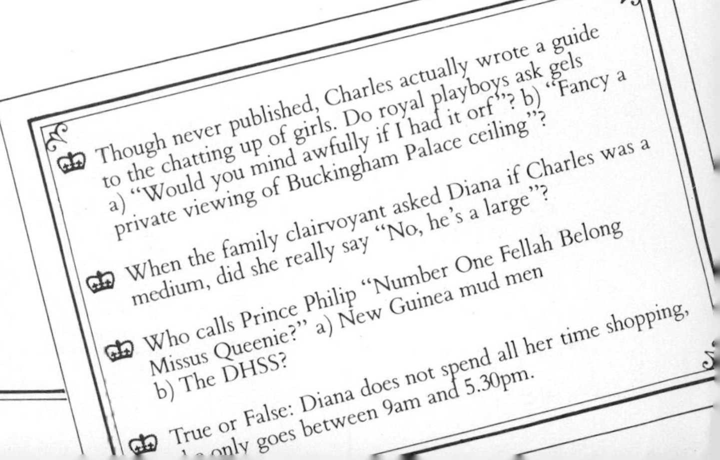

- Though never published, Charles actually wrote a guide to the chatting up of girls. Do royal playboys ask gels a) "Would you mind awfully if I had it orf"? b) "Fancy a private viewing of Buckingham Palace ceiling"?
- When the family clairvoyant asked Diana if Charles was a medium, did she really say "No, he's a large"?
- Who calls Prince Philip "Number One Fellah Belong Missus Queenie?" a) New Guinea mud men b) The DHSS?
- True or False: Diana does not spend all her time shopping, ... only goes between 9am and 5.30pm.

EUROPE
on Ten Dresses a Day

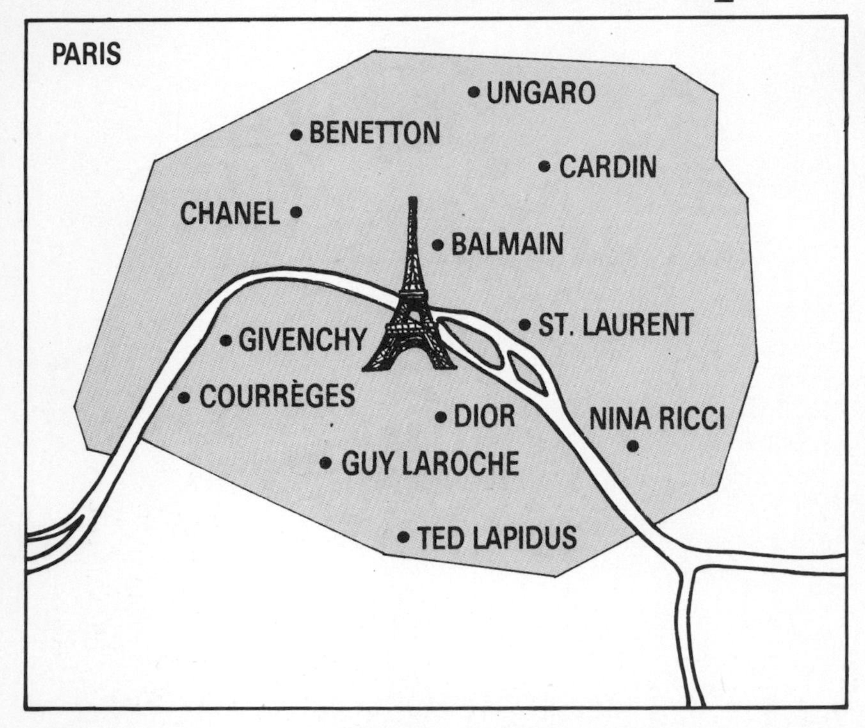

FRANCE

POPULATION: 39,000,001
NUMERO DE COIFFEURS: 47,284

Palaces worth Visiting

VERSAILLES

Di's rating
"Not bad considering there's no disco, but I adored all those mirrors. Fine for a budget tour; most suites are under £2000 a night."

THE LOUVRE

Di says
"Always makes me giggle. I mean 'Louvre' sounds so like 'loo'! Tee-hee . . . Just like all those Froggy chappies going 'wee-wee' all day! Mind you, they didn't have any paintings of me. . ."

A Soupcon de Frog

"We were appalled at the number of French people who couldn't understand our accents. Even more than the number of English! So, Sarah and I have been swotting up for our next ski trip."

Froggy	English
"Tant pis"	"My aunt is drunk" (Use this phrase quite a lot)
"C'est si bon!"	"There's the singer from Duran Duran!"
"C'est la vie!"	"There's the lavatory!"
"Menu prix complet"	"Menu for complete pricks"

Di's Diary

LUNDI: Until we got to Paris, I thought Norman Mailer was an old French letter! Which reminds me, why do the Froggies correspond on pieces of rubber?

MARDI: It's always smashing to visit somewhere with some real history. Do you realise that the Eiffel Tower actually appeared in the last James Bond film as well as the Duran Duran video?

MERCREDI: Guess what?! Le Bon is actually a Froggie name. We heard someone singing about him today ... "Sur le Bon d'Avignon". I think it means "on top of Simon having one."

JEUDI: SUPER NEWS! the Froggies have ended nearly every day of the week with my name!! They're a peculiar lot though ... this vicar got all upset when I said Sacré Blue Cathedral reminded us of the Taj Mahal. What's wrong with the Taj?

VENDREDI: Extraordinary! All the magazine covers have got that awful Caroline on, not me! Her fashion sense is appalling. She never wears Guernseys or Barbours! Perhaps I should give one of the Frogs a kiss ... it worked last time! Hee hee!!!

SAMEDI: "Quel fromage!" as they say, we have to leave tomorrow and thousands of people haven't seen me! Still we have tried some of the local food. Last night we had 'French Fries', 'Moulons Marinière' and things called 'Cretins' in our soup.

DIMANCHE: The Di I went on the channel. I asked Charles why there are so many cross-channel ferries, never any friendly ones. He tried to shoot himself. Again!

(*) POSTCARD LIST

- ✓ Bob & Paula
- ✓ Sir Dickie A.
- ✓ Sir Alastair B.

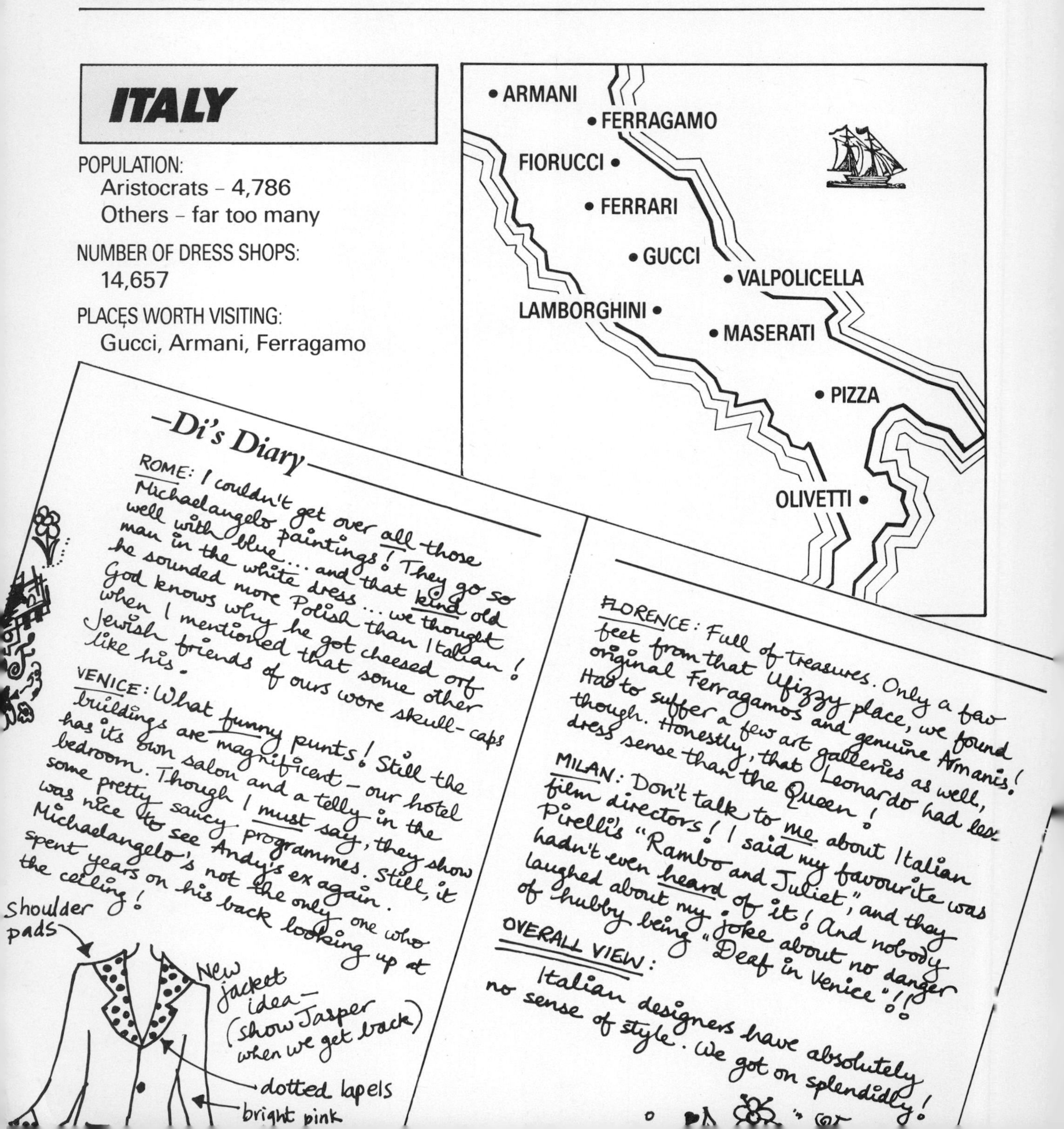
ITALY
POPULATION:
Aristocrats – 4,786
Others – far too many
NUMBER OF DRESS SHOPS:
14,657
PLACES WORTH VISITING:
Gucci, Armani, Ferragamo
ARMANI
FERRAGAMO
FIORUCCI
FERRARI
GUCCI
VALPOLICELLA
LAMBORGHINI
MASERATI
PIZZA
OLIVETTI
—Di's Diary—
ROME: I couldn't get over all those Michaelangelo paintings! They go so well with blue... and that kind old man in the white dress... we thought he sounded more Polish than Italian! God knows why he got cheesed off when I mentioned that some other Jewish friends of ours wore skull-caps like his.
VENICE: What funny punts! Still the buildings are magnificent – our hotel has its own salon and a telly in the bedroom. Though I must say, they show some pretty saucy programmes. Still, it was nice to see Andy's ex again. Michaelangelo's not the only one who spent years on his back looking up at the ceiling!
Shoulder pads
New jacket idea – (show Jasper when we get back)
dotted lapels
bright pink
FLORENCE: Full of treasures. Only a few feet from that Ufizzy place, we found original Ferragamos and genuine Armanis! Had to suffer a few art galleries as well, though. Honestly, that Leonardo had less dress sense than the Queen!
MILAN: Don't talk to me about Italian film directors! I said my favourite was Pirelli's "Rambo and Juliet," and they hadn't even heard of it! And nobody laughed about my joke about no danger of hubby being "Deaf in Venice"!!
OVERALL VIEW:
Italian designers have absolutely no sense of style. We got on splendidly!

If that's your IQ, or your salary in millions, you'll love a holiday aboard...

BRITANNIA CRUISES

See only the rich bits of the world — real castles on the sand — lively knightspots — far from the maddening crowds of riffraff and German tourists. You won't even have to take your own holiday snaps — the world's press will do that for you. For a distorted view of foreign countries in the company of a fun bunch of people with IQs of 18-30, book a Britannia cruise today!

You're guaranteed a GAY TIME!

Yes, here on the largest yacht in the world, nine of the boys were jailed for opening a homosexual vice ring. And you can still see one or two of the "Petticoat Officers" frolicking about in their traditional navy knickers, pop socks, serge blouses and matching hair-bands. So come and join the sport of queens with the "Snotty yachties" — book a Britannia cruise today, boys — there's a rear-admiral who'd love to take you up on his bridge!

Heirobics*

You know, you too could have a body like Di. In which case you'd look pretty scrawny. See if these exercises can help...

EAROBICS

1. Ears forward

2. Ears back

3. Ears relaxed

THE LADY DI OR "DUMB BELLE"

Great for stretching the neck muscles and the national deficit. Just wear heavy diamonds on your headband as often as possible

1. EXERCISING ONE'S PREROGATIVE

And bend, two, three, four,
And kneel, two, three, four,
Bow the head, two, three, four,
And knight, two, three, four
and relax

2. EXERCISES FOR ALL THE FAMILY

* Taken from the forthcoming book **"KEEP THICK WITH DI"**

The First Di Cover

How to be a Royal Wally

Charles demonstrates the correct way of picking one's nose with the Welsh National Emblem

Every officer has his rank marked on his parachute

"And they said Sinclair was bonkers..."

Charles helps a soldier to stuff a flagpole down his trousers

"Is that what you call cocked?"

"I am a countryman, a country bumpkin"

– OUR NEXT KING QUOTED IN 1985

Rapidly approaching his 40th birthday, a helicopter pilot wonders if he can still get it up

Play Doll Collection

* Stay trim after all those state banquets with *My Little Princesses®'* personal stereo and aerobics kit.

More vacant than Barbie, more silly than Cindy, *My Little Princess®* is every uneducated girl's dream.

★ And now you can join her on her many adventures in a complete fantasy world, totally different from the real surroundings poor people have to live in.

★ Take your princess to a fabulously expensive wedding. Spend a week trying on her vast collection of dresses. Or simply sit your Princess in front of her countless vanity mirrors.

★ *My Little Princess®* comes complete with thousands of exciting wigs, dyes, combs, curlers and sprays providing hour upon hour of the 'hairplay' so many little girls love, and only one or two over-privileged big girls get to make a career of.

★ And just look at these unique action movements! *My Little Princess®* can actually wave her hand and adjust her fringe at the same time! Great!

★ Her handsome beau, *Action Prince®*, can actually wiggle those ears too! Providing endless hours of 'ear- play'.

★ And now that *My Little Prince®* has come, *My Little Princess®* proudly presents her very own royal baby doll collection. Not only do these beautiful royal babes come complete with self-wetting nappy sets so you too can experience a royal wee, there's also a whole range of *Action Nanny®* dolls fully equipped to rescue *My Little Princess®* from any of the everyday chores that normal mothers have to suffer.

* Give *Action Prince®* a blonde wig and a poncy overall, and he's your little Princess's very own personal coiffeur!

* Hours of fun with *My Little Princesses®'* wigs, combs, sprays and other exciting hair-play accessories.

★ GIVE YOUR LITTLE GIRLS COMPLETE DELUSIONS OF GRANDEUR . . . .

* Just pull *My Little Princess's*® string of pearls and she will say *"okay yar"* and giggle incessantly!
Super new nose sets. Collect them **all**
A GENUINE HEIR-PLAY PRODUCT
* No-bend knees — *They curtsey to you!*
Every doll guaranteed just as plastic as the real thing

WITH THE MY LITTLE PRINCESS® PLAY-DOLL COLLECTION FROM HEIR-PLAY

Available at a Late Learning Centre near you

ROYAL EXPOSURES

The Queen at 60

"I like to expose myself"

"I reckon all great photographers should be like the top girls, keen on handling their own prints, as it were... That Lord Letchfield has helped me pick up all sorts. Taught me a bit about photography as well..."

LETCHFIELD says:

"I'd recommend calendar work. When you're as rich as us, you can even take your own photographer."

DAVID DAILY says:

"Well, John, I fink he'd get much better results if he left the lens cap on. Mind you, once you realize that the blurr is in fact the Queen...

The night of my honeymoon

Worghh, I had fun touching this one up, the picture that is! I thought why not give her a flash and see what develops ... CORR, I thought I'd turned into a tripod

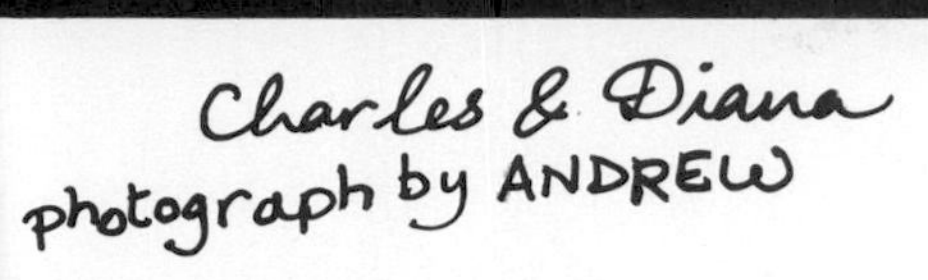

Charles & Diana
photograph by ANDREW

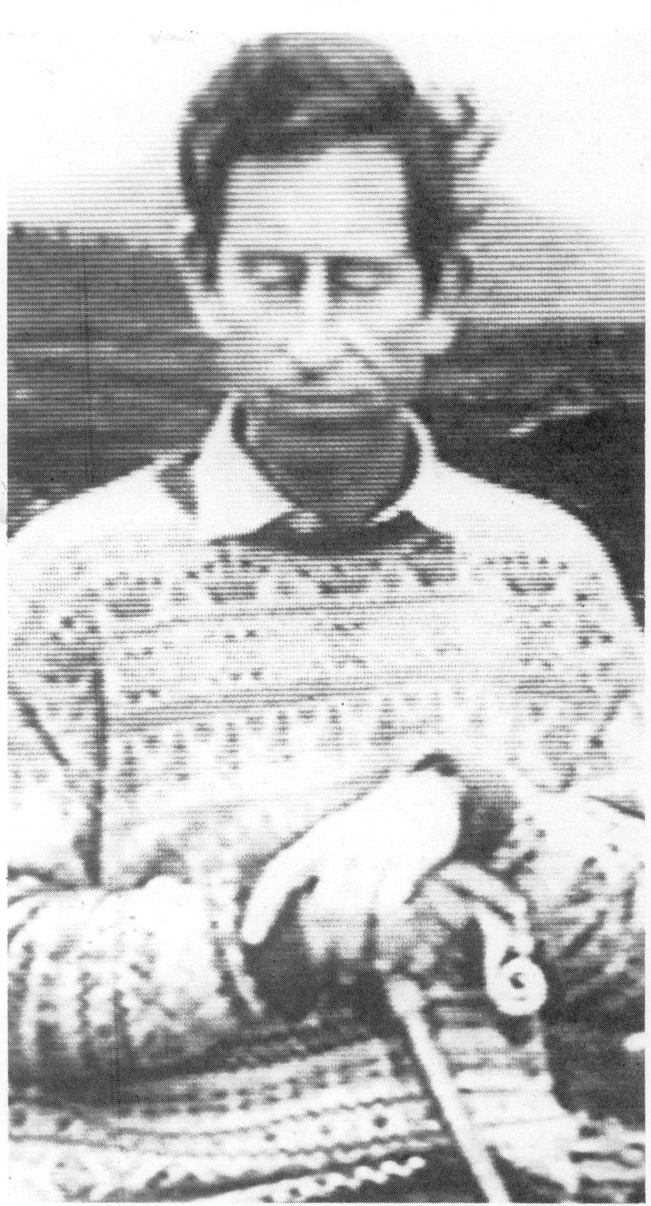

CHARLES ↑
or possibly EDWARD

Blimey, you should have seen my
F-stop when I caught sight of her apertures!

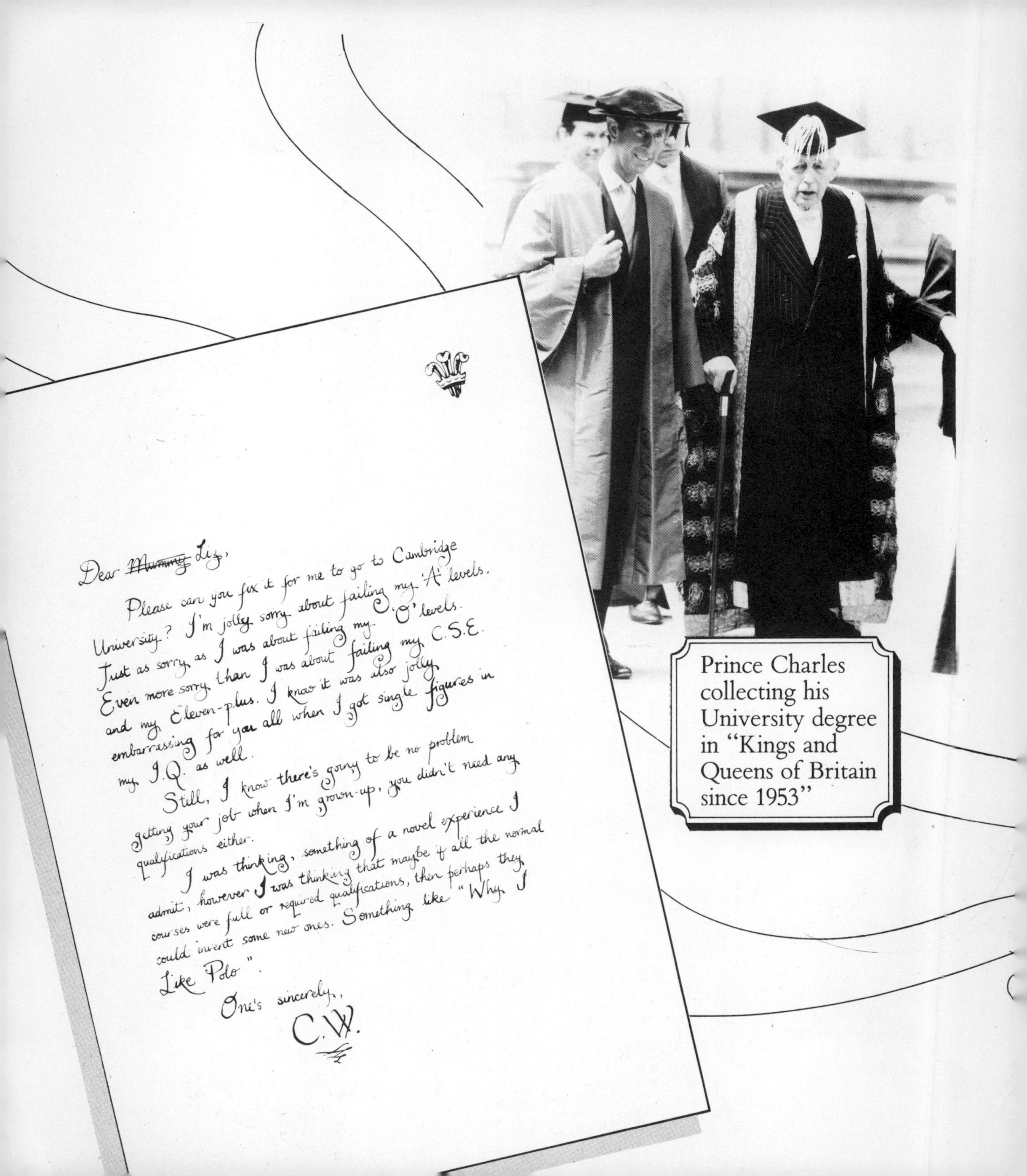

Dear ~~Mummy~~ Liz,

Please can you fix it for me to go to Cambridge University? I'm jolly sorry about failing my 'A' levels. Just as sorry as I was about failing my 'O' levels. Even more sorry than I was about failing my C.S.E. and my Eleven-plus. I know it was also jolly embarrassing for you all when I got single figures in my I.Q. as well.

Still, I know there's going to be no problem getting your job when I'm grown-up, you didn't need any qualifications either.

I was thinking, something of a novel experience I admit, however I was thinking that maybe if all the normal courses were full or required qualifications, then perhaps they could invent some new ones. Something like "Why I Like Polo".

One's sincerely,

C.W.

Prince Charles collecting his University degree in "Kings and Queens of Britain since 1953"

Dear Liz,

Please can you fix it for me to go to the Royal Collidge of Art? I have dun quite a bit of painting, well painting by numbers actually. Well auction numbers in fact, but still, I've read the prospectus for the Royal Collage or Royal Academy or whatever it's called, and it's a perfectly acceptable address. I know all the places are supposed to have gone and everything, but loads of the people they've taken are just rif- raf. I mean lots of them are just art students, and God knows you can't get much tattier than that. Half of them can't even afford Burberry's!

So please, Aunty, could you see your way clear.......

Lots of love and kisses, S.

COMPLETE COINCIDENCE: Lady Sarah Armstrong-Jones, the Queen's niece, was admitted to the Royal College of Art in 1985, after the full quota of college places had been taken.

Dear Liz,

Please could you transform an unqualified sloane into an international cover girl? Just a few hundred grand on stylists could do the trick.

Please could you also fix it for me to meet all my fave pop stars, dance with my fave film stars, live in a palace and one day get your job?

P.S. I'm also a bit worried about my nose...

AND LIZ FIXED IT!

An old fart in a wet suit

Royal men do eat quiche

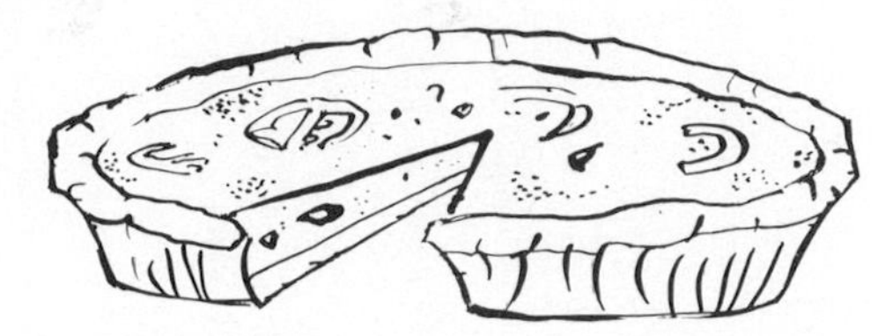

Whatever happened to turn Action Man into a vegetarian?

Royal men should feast on the spoils of blood-sports, not sunflower-seed flapjacks.

Royal men shouldn't worry about concrete jungles; simply about getting the lion's share.

Royal men should swig hip-flasks not sip decaffeinated tea.

Royal landowners should take potshots at trespassers, not offer guides to local walks.

Royal Cornishmen should demand Mayday fertility rites of local wenches, not encourage wickerwork and pottery co-operatives.

Royal princes should play strip poker, not Tarot and Ouija.

Royal princes should dwell on inner thighs, not inner cities and the inner self.

Royal men should join the Marines, not the Morris-dancers.

Royal men don't have to justify their existence;

Royal men believe in Divine Right with all the perks.

Royal men should be called "Lionheart", not Charlie.

But today's Royal man eats quiche...

Anne would have made a much better man for the job!

"Few chaps realize that one of the Monarch's prerogatives is to turn every parish in the land into a University. I hope that alternative Cornwall will teach us all to live in a kingdom full of peace, harmony and regular bowel movements".

– MAHARISHI CHARLIE

PROPOSED ROUTE OF CORNISH CHANNEL TUNNEL

BLACK HEAD
Not a very nice spot. Similar to Meverpussy

GOONHILLY CENTRE FOR COLLECTING COSMIC VIBES
Quite apart from gathering all things "cosmic" and "spaced-out" Goonhilly's famous radar dishes are used by the prince's wife for projecting episodes of "Dynasty" and "Emmerdale Farm" around the world

PENZANCE PIRATE RADIO
Plays non-stop sea-shanties with a disco backing

FOULMOUTH COLLEGE
Where they teach you to swear like a sailor and make horrible jokes about discharged seamen in naval bases

Legend has it that King Arthur and the Nits of the Round Table named this place after their sidekick Merlin. Merlin came to these parts to buy extra top hats, wands, and the occasional new TV gameshow idea from America

THE WIZARD

TREVOMIT COLLEGE OF ORGANIC COOKERY

Inner Cities

THE NEEDLES ACUPUNCTURE CENTRE

WENCHPOKE CENTRE FOR ASSERTIVE TRAINING
Now owned by the National Thrust, Wenchpoke offers Summer Schools in Est, Finding Yourself and Getting-the-easily-influenced-to-share-their-money

THE NOODLES
Wholefood College. Phds in Bowel movements and Wind Development. Many students suffer expulsion

REST OF THE WORLD

CALLINGTON
Where conservationist Charles ordered three acres of trees to be chopped down because they disturbed the rare "Heath Fritillary" butterfly. Was this simply to prove that he was not prejudiced against cocoons?

MILLION COVE
Another fantastically expensive holiday estate provided for the prince and princess's use by a publicity-hungry American millionaire

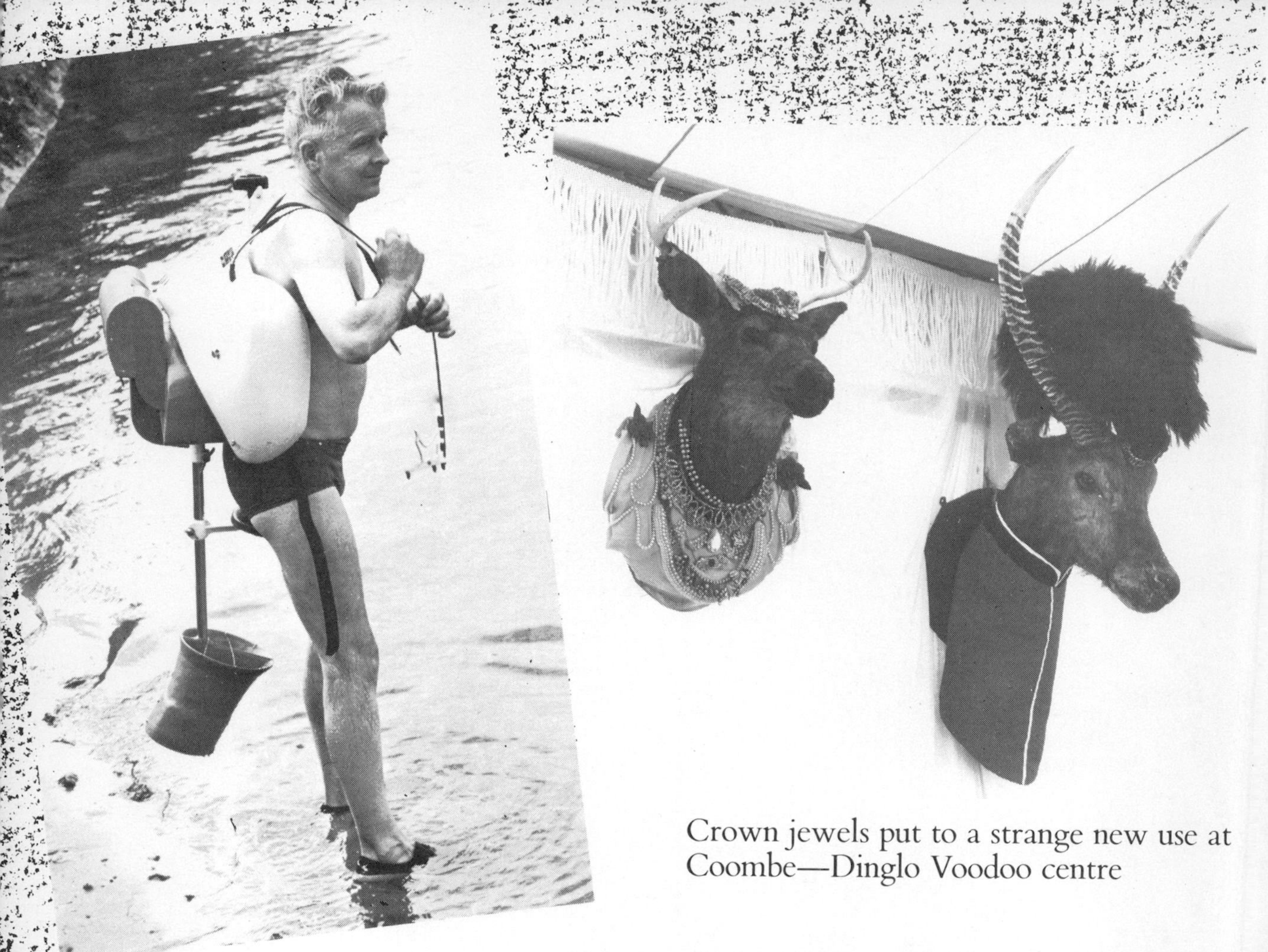

Crown jewels put to a strange new use at Coombe—Dinglo Voodoo centre

This year's winner of the Duke of Cornwally award, Dan Fartalot, the frogman who flipped

Two village idiots from Lower Dingle—o College of Alternative Agriculture and Knitting try to speed up milk delivery by crossing a bull with a milk float. (The man seated now wears an eyepatch.)

Students at Polperro's new "Save-the-barmy-pigmy" society

Students at Trebigdick Technical Cottage studying Fertility Rites and Rock Erection

Maharishi Son—Miss—Queenie—White—man casting out evil possessions with Karmachanics

Exclusive preview of Charles' own plans for the new look inner-cities of his kingdom to come.

Out go glass stumps and monstrous carbuncles, in comes Chuls' own neo-Laurens van der post-modern-Georgio-mock rococco-Mies van der Thatch-Carolingian-neo Sloane.

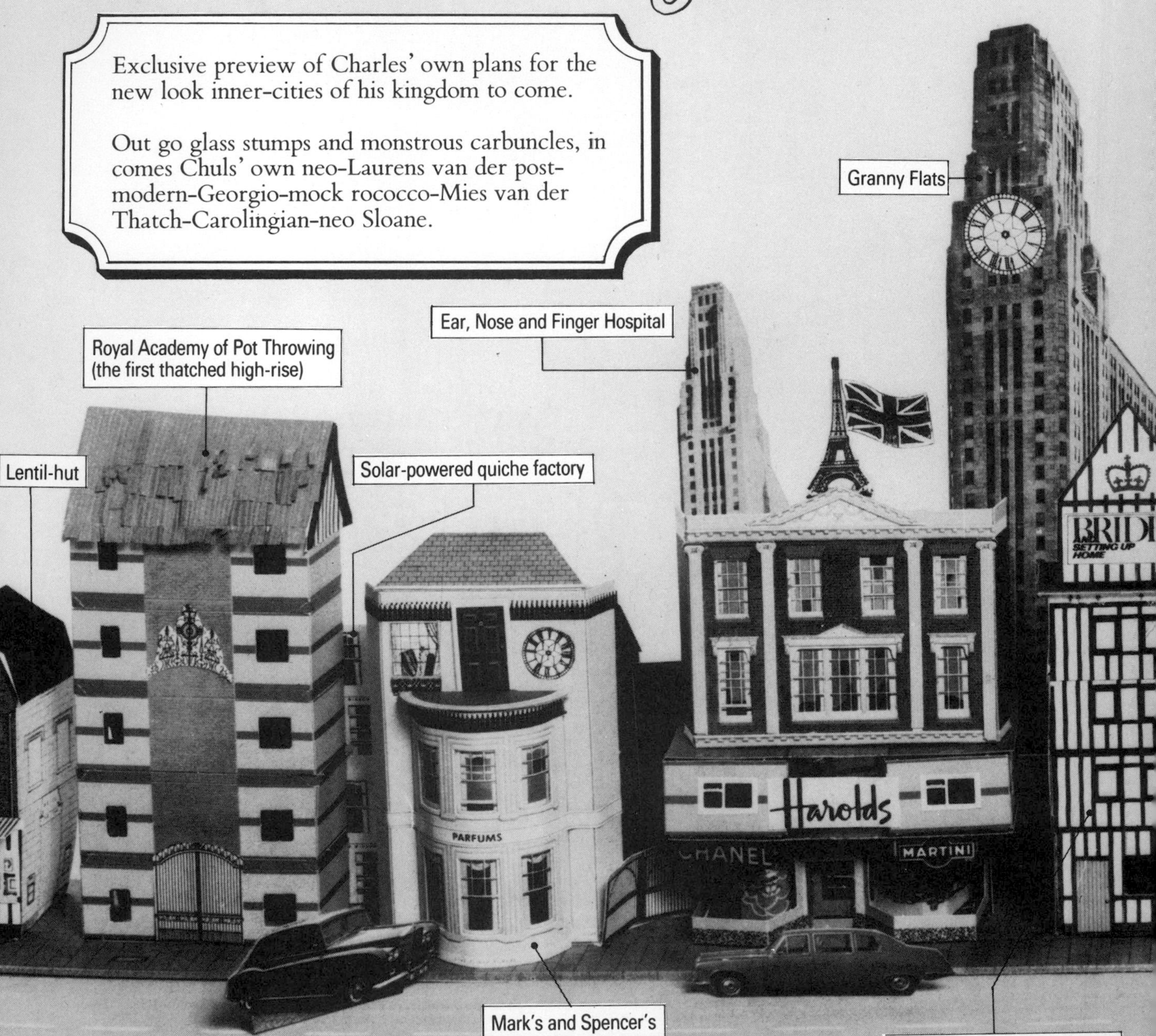

Andy helicopter pad
Sir John Betjeman writes
"Looks pretty good from where I am"
Cranks
MARRIAGE BUREAUX
Was Henry VIII a Flying Saucer? research centre
Matercare
Royal Bank of Cornwall
GARBARD
The Crown Jewellers
PRIDE
One's Price Records
Place for those young unemployed chaps to do all sorts of useful things

FROM GORDONSTOUN RUGBY CLUB ★ DEAR FERGIE ★ FROM ONE "GOOD TEAM" TO ANOTHER ★
WE FOUND HIM TERRIFIC IN EVERY POSITION
HOPE YOU DO TOO! ★ ★ ★
RomaNcing The SloaNe
SHE LIKES:
"His wit, his charm, the large space between his ears, and getting a bigger ring than what Di got."
Prince and Princess Randy
Just two ordinary heirs to the throne very much in love
HE LIKES:
"Her red hair, her Marty Feldman impressions and the extra £30,000 a year."
FROM BCK GRAPHICS ★ I KNOW WE SAID YOU SHOULD MAKE YOUR OWN PRINTS, BUT THIS IS RIDICULOUS! ★
FROM KOO, CAROLYN, GEMMA, KIM, KATIE, VICKI, CLARE, FINOLA AND KIRSTY ET AL★ANDY DARLING★PROMIS

FROM PADDY MACWALLY*FERGIE, MY LITTLE RACER*WHEN YOU WERE ON THE CIRCUIT ALL OF ME WAS RACING*NOW IT'S THE PITS*PLEASE GIVE ME ONE LAST CLUTCH ... * * *

Major Froggie's speech ...

Your Majesty-in-law, Chaps and Chapesses,

Heard news filly of mine tieing knot with Randy...so excited, I flew to Australia...

Don't mind telling you, this one's a real man. Sort of chap who pulls his finger out instead of chopping it orf! Papers asked me I my gel was up to it. I told 'em. Said she never had any trouble controlling first pony, shouldn't have any bother with new stud either. He's my sort of chap.... unbelievably thick. Anyway, taught Johhny Argie a lesson...Not so much losing a daughter as gaining a Duke of York. Don't have to fork out wedding either. Apparently, got fair bit in common with m you know, two eyes, too many teeth and ridiculously plummy accent...Papers say she's more sophisticated than Diana. So what? So's Noddy! Anyway, the Daily Mail prints a load of crap...

GALTIERI-GRAM * GALTIERI-GRAM * GALTIERI-GRAM * GA

DEAR PRINCE ANDY, SORRY WE MISSED YOU IN THE FALKLANDS * STILL, MY AMIGO SENOR BARRANTES, HE SAY YOU MAKE GREAT CATCH, SO PLEASE TO COME AND STAY AS MY ~~PRISONERS~~ GUESTS IN ARGENTINA * * * *

* * * * * * * * *

Buckingham Palace

SPECIAL NOTICE

"What a Pair"

The palace considers it absolutely disgusting to display pictures of Andy and Fergie in public. All T-shirts will therefore be banned. Andy and Fergie nasal decongestants and Andy and Fergie odour eaters must also be kept well hidden

YOU WON'T TAKE HER ANYWHERE YOU'VE BEEN WITH US*P.S. HAVE A NICE TIME IN SKEGNESS*STOP *

ROYAL TOURS

On earlier trips to Australia, Charles always used to wear headlights to excite the Sheilas

AFRICA

According to the highly-informative "Royal Book of Lists", when the Queen was travelling in a horse-drawn carriage with an African ruler, one of the horses farted. *"I'm so sorry"*, said Her Majesty, at which the African replied, *"Oh, don't worry, if you hadn't apologised, I'd have thought it was the horse"*.

"Hello dere, brudders. Dis am Miss Queenie White man speakin', com all dee way from Miss Queenie land in big silver bird. Please be tellin' dee big twit wid dee umbrella dat it's only me who am reigning!"

PAPUA NEW GUINEA

The Washington Dinner

Guests included

1 Ronald Reagan, (*creator of the Star Wars plan, whereby old stars get to start wars*).
2 Nancy Reagan.
3 Princess "David".
4 HRH Prince Chuck.
5 Reagan's diplomatic advisor and chief of nukes.
6 Peter Ustinov or the British Ambassador.
7 John Travolta.
8 Mayor of Carmel.
9 Joan Collins.
10 Joan Rivers.
11 Woolly Allen.

No longer by Royal Appointment

ROYAL CRORSSWORD

"ACRORSS"

1 Prince that can be a prick (5).

3 Flasher sounds like he got caught in a blizzard (7).

6 What one can never have at state functions (1).

7 Goes with ender of the faith and Di's spelling of hard of hearing (3).

9 As secret society member Philip should be stoned (5).

13 Responsible for hereditary characteristics, including inane grins (3).

15 The most intelligent thing Mark ever said (2).

17 & 21 In a roundabout way "Mein father once pick SS" added to a learner (8, 7, 2, 4).

19 Between God and my right and reminds us of Margaret (2).

20 Anagram of UE (2).

21 See 17.

25 Di's "O" level total belongs in a convent (4).

26 What Philip probably calls the Pope (3).

28 Di's "O" Levels

29 US port in storm in which Margaret can be found (6).

30 What Charles may well be in the reign (3).

32 What the palace should put on Di's monotonous publicity (3).

33 Exactly like Duke of Edinburgh (4, 2, 9).

36 How Di spells cold (2).

37 Religious teaching with which Queen sees (2).

38 Brief description of Michael's pa describes Mark at his brightest (3).

39 Do you like the Royal Family? (2).

40 Anne's doctor (3).

41 Philip or one who's dry after initial beverage (4).

42 Like jungle or royal heads (5).

43 Henry's wives or doodlebug (2).

44 Backward princess seen by psychiatrists (2).

45 Backward queen (2).

46 Bo Derek or Andy's IQ (3).

47 How Princess Michael describes herself and start to Charlie's motto (3).

48 Amin's other half reversed to describe Philip (5).

49 When corgis lift legs as queen describes herself (2).

50 Product of Cornish mines forged to describe their owner (3).

51 The only useful thing Buckingham palace gives the public (1).

"DINE"

1 What Charles has become to start hamburger chain (4).

2 Jungle ruler that's tamer than Mark (4).

3 Something Philip has never made (5).

4 Letters to represent what they are abroad and party Princess Michael may belong to (2).

5 Pupil with Di's initial appropriately on its hat (5).

8 What Danny La Rue speaks when he's not being improper (6, 7).

10 Royal Academy turned upside down to describe Farmer Charles' philosophy on life (2).

11 What Di makes so many feel (4).

12 How Andy spells his favourite make of camera (4).

13 Sounds like artificial hair colourant and needs it too (2).

14 Similar to Farmer Charles' word of wisdom in 10 (2).

16 About the only thing that's more stuck up than the royals (4).

18 Randy's favourite show (5).

21 Where lefties want monarchs (3).

22 Elizabeth's letters sound like making mistake (2).

23 Small birds main focus of Andy's lens (3).

24 To crown it all, here's a street where the Windsors would be intellectually out of depth (10).

27 How Di spells teacher (5).

29 Rhymes with and looks like Di clone (5).

30 Andy's Falklands situation makes what Koo's often seen in backwards (3).

31 What they do to the throne but never at school (7).

32 Unlike Andy, Charles once said "I am not accustomed to unveiling . . .s" (4).

34 Ruler's right to succession as gross pop queen (6).

35 Anagram of SB. (2).

42 How Di spells opposite of 30 acrorss (3).

43 How Di spells scene from window (3).

47 Do Andy and Sarah do this? (2).

WHO'S WHO?

Can you recognize the Royals?

1 **Just fill in the famous names beneath the famous hands.**
For instance, if you think hands **A** belong to Charles, put Charles. If you think they belong to Andy, put Andy. It's so simple you could do it with your hands tied behind your back.

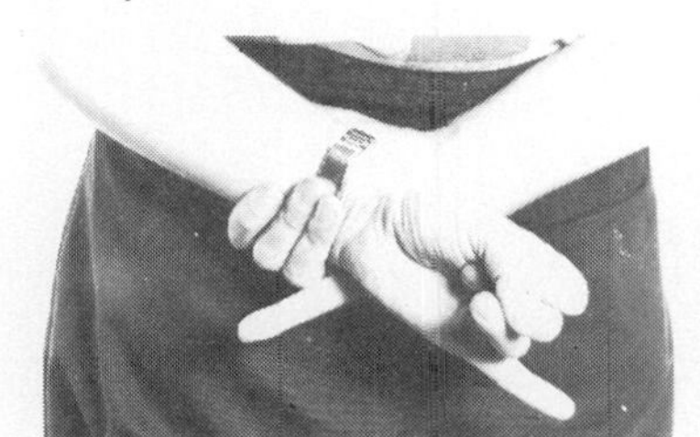

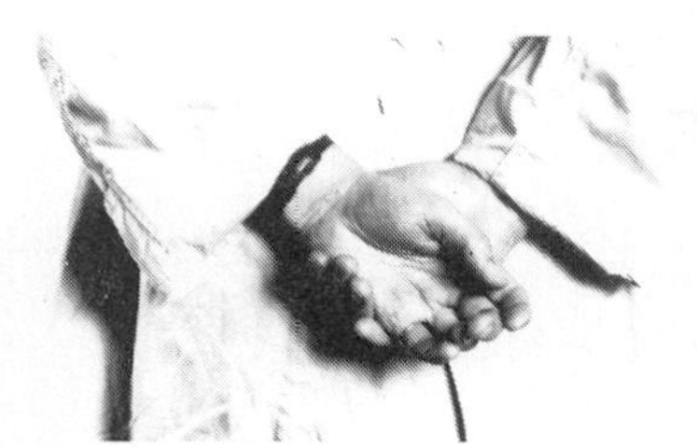

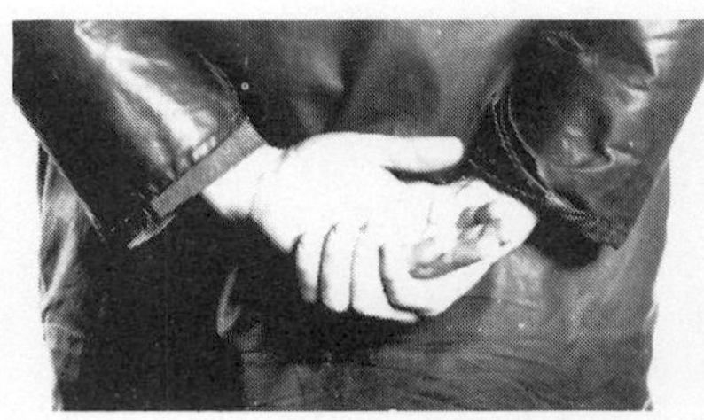

A _________________ **B** _________________ **C** _________________

2 **Just fill in the famous royal ladies' names beneath the correct hands.**
For instance, if you can see whisky stains on glove **A**, write Margaret. If you see horse manure, write Anne.

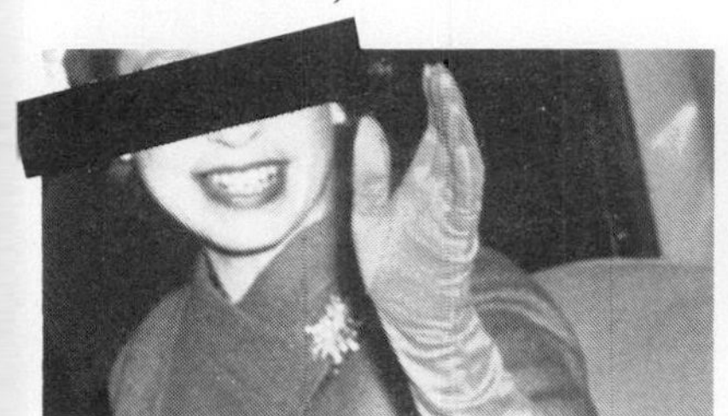

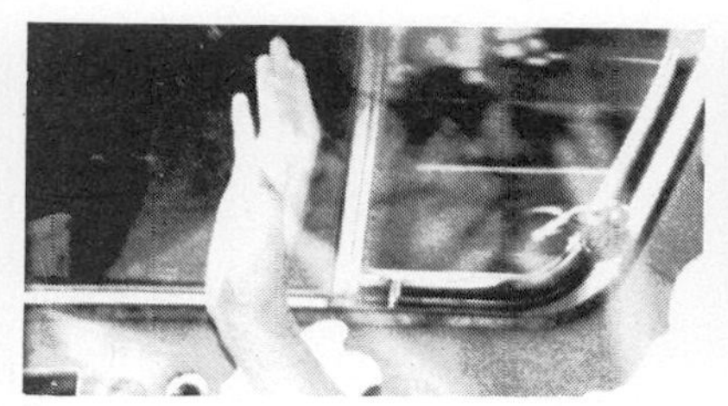

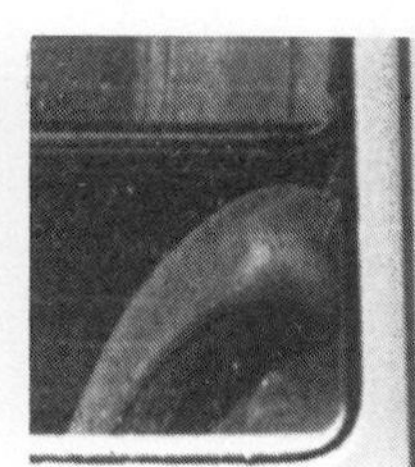

A _________________ **B** _________________ **C** _________________

3 **Just fill in the family names beneath their incredibly fixed grins.**
For instance, if you think **B** is the biggest mouth in Britain, write Philip. If you think **C** is the most inane thing you've ever seen, put Di.

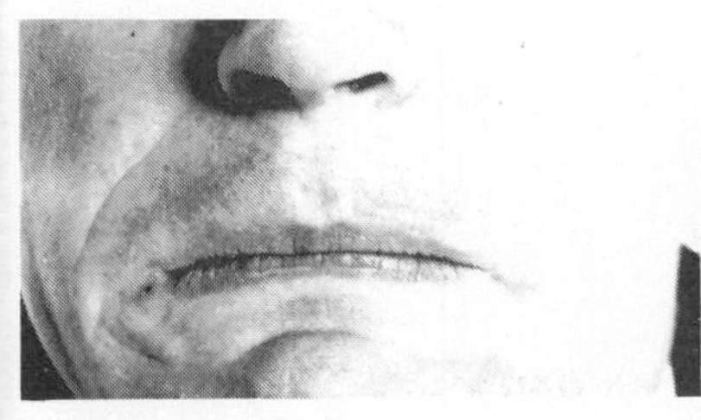

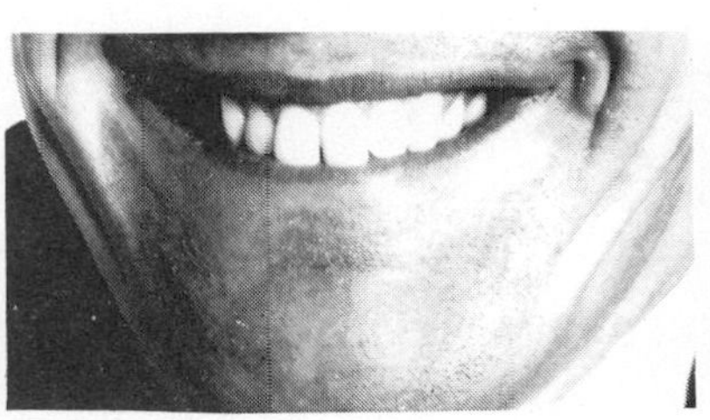

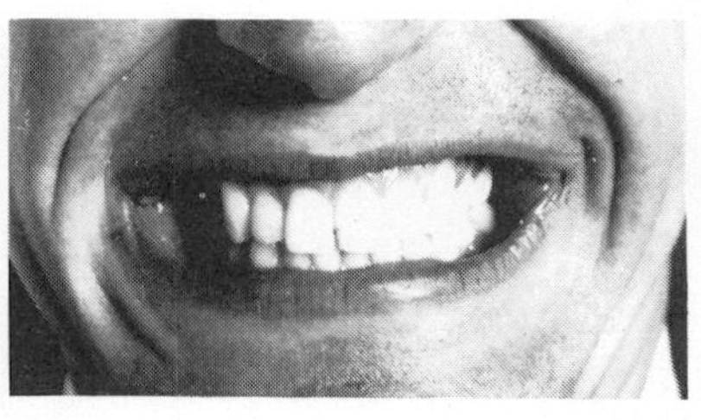

A _________________ **B** _________________ **C** _________________

FOR SALE

BUCKINGHAM PALACE

Would suit family of six with 400 staff. 600 recep., give or take a hundred, lake, cinema, double-carriage, commanding views, but OWNERS BADLY IN NEED OF MODERNISATION.

THE PROPERTY: A well proportioned detached palace, ideal for a family that like to give themselves heirs. Present owners possess many mod cons, particularly that of conning the public into paying all their household bills.

LOCATION: Situated in pleb-free zone within easy reach of tiara servicers. Actually built on the site of an old sewer, though this never causes anything like the stink when people discover that the property comes complete with 121 "grace and favour" properties the owners can dish out to friends and relatives.

OTHER FEATURES: The sunny, 40-acre rear garden could be sold for billions as central London office space, but the present owners like to keep it on for tea parties. There is a private tube line to Heathrow and a fallout shelter where one of the present owner's sons keeps his hair.

ACCOMMODATION COMPRISES: Ample stabling for household cavalry, feature 153ft through-gallery, numerous low-flush thrones, easy-access master bedroom, dungeon, nanny estates and gyms, never-used utility room and planning permission for anything you like - Owners may grant it themselves.

The property includes a Summer House, a Winter Palace, an Autumn Estate and a Spring county.

** VIEWING STRICTLY BY ROYAL APPOINTMENT **

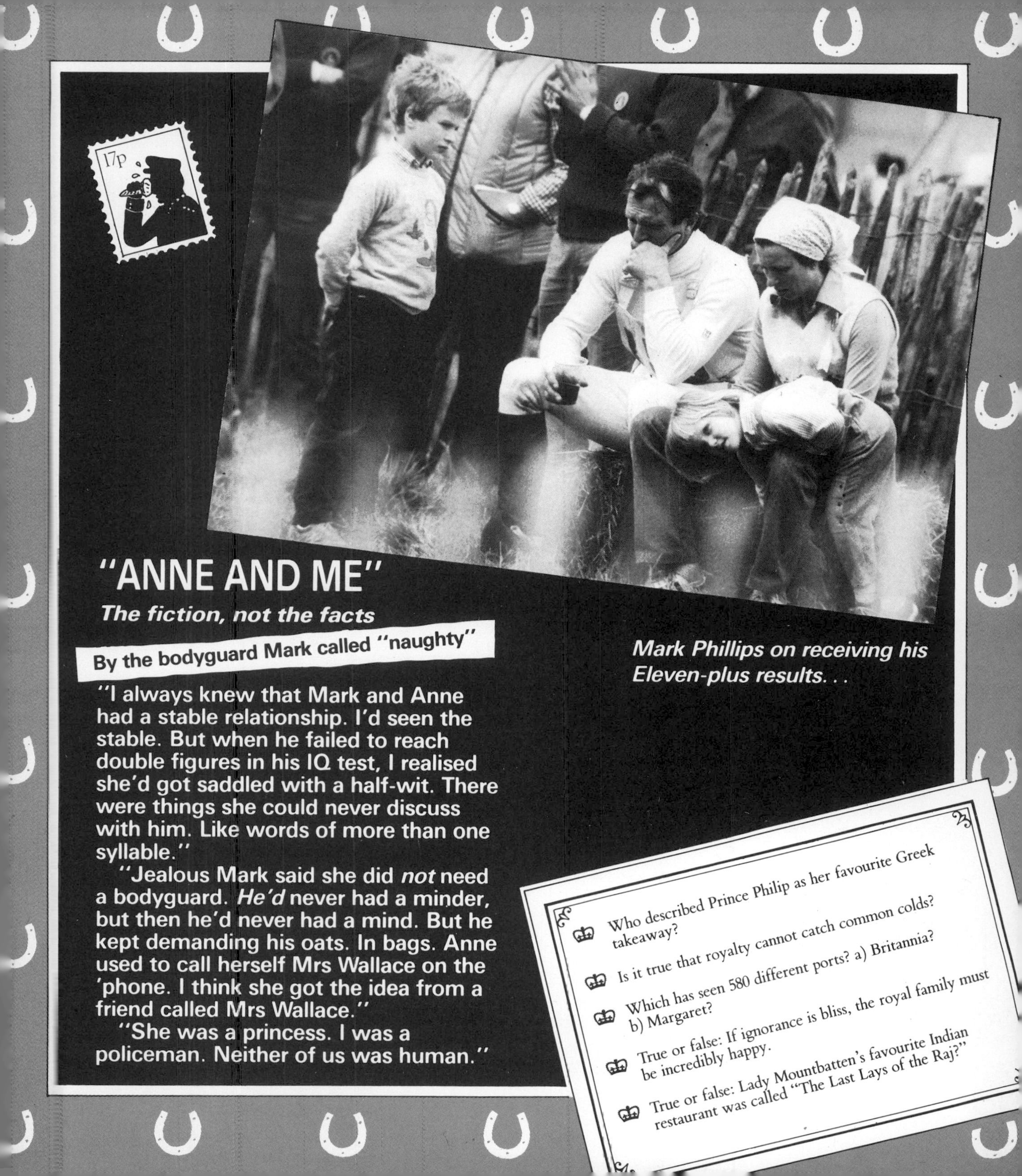

Mark Phillips on receiving his Eleven-plus results. . .

"ANNE AND ME"

The fiction, not the facts

By the bodyguard Mark called "naughty"

"I always knew that Mark and Anne had a stable relationship. I'd seen the stable. But when he failed to reach double figures in his IQ test, I realised she'd got saddled with a half-wit. There were things she could never discuss with him. Like words of more than one syllable."

"Jealous Mark said she did *not* need a bodyguard. *He'd* never had a minder, but then he'd never had a mind. But he kept demanding his oats. In bags. Anne used to call herself Mrs Wallace on the 'phone. I think she got the idea from a friend called Mrs Wallace."

"She was a princess. I was a policeman. Neither of us was human."

- Who described Prince Philip as her favourite Greek takeaway?
- Is it true that royalty cannot catch common colds?
- Which has seen 580 different ports? a) Britannia? b) Margaret?
- True or false: If ignorance is bliss, the royal family must be incredibly happy.
- True or false: Lady Mountbatten's favourite Indian restaurant was called "The Last Lays of the Raj?"

Relatives one doesn't like to mention

How come they're basically all krauts? Is this why today's royals all say "Okay ja?"

How come we allowed George of Hanover to become king anyway? From his first day as George I to the day he become George the stiff, he didn't speak a word of English. Like so many after him, he was totally out of touch with the rest of the country.

Even Philip's real surname is Schleswig-Holstein-Sonderburg-Glucksburg, and he claims to be Greek. Whoever heard of Zorba the Schleswig-Holstein-Sonderburg-Glucksburg? Philip's ancestors obviously got inbred with a few famous lagers.

In 1914, when George V had to admit that he was Kaiser Bill's cousin, the royals rapidly changed their surname from the not too British "Saxe-Coburg" to "Windsor". They also swapped the previously traditional dachshunds for corgis, which are a similar size but don't wear armbands.

Mind you, Oliver Cromwell's about the only person who's ever questioned the monarchy. Under Henry III, we let ourselves be ruled by a nine-year old. Under Edward VI, by a ten-year old. Later William of Orange, and coming soon, Charles who's going bananas.

Along the way, much interbonking created such twits as James I, the pillock who actually knighted a loin of beef, which thereafter became known as "Sir Loin". He also displayed more cod pieces than Birds Eye! But he had nothing on George III . . .

Kaiser Bill demonstrates his skill as a parrot tamer

GEORGE III 1738-1820

They don't come much barmier than George III! Following his mother's particularly shrewd advice *"Be a King George"*, George became a king and promptly lost his marbles. On one particular occasion he actually spent some considerable time talking to what he thought was the French ambassador but later turned out to be an oak tree!

When he went barmy every day, the politicians did something even barmier — a Whig called Ponsonby, (sounds like one of Jeremy Thorpe's ancestors), suggested making the then Prince of Wales Prince Regent. Look what happened . . .

GEORGE IV 1762-1830

"He wanted, as his father had often wanted, a broad-bottomed administration", said one eminent historian. Dead right, Georgie Boy was bent as a nine-bob note. Show him a "broad-bottomed administration" and he'd guarantee they had all their members behind them in a flash. Literally!

George IV enjoys a light snack

Convinced that "Primogeniture" meant "having first-class genitals", Georgie boy endeavoured to display them to as many people as possible. If Brighton is now considered the gay capital of Europe, George IV should really be considered its first Queen.

INCREDIBLE
-But true!

Lady Di is actually related to all of the following:

THE MARQUIS DE SADE (Double Fourth Cousin Seven Times Removed)
Can't you detect the infliction of pain and mental suffering on Charles every time she opens her mouth?

LORD LUCAN (Second Cousin Once Removed).
Also, Nanny permanently removed, and quite possibly others too. This man specialized in removing people, including himself.

LOUISA M. ALCOTT (Seventh Cousin Four times Removed)
Author of "Little Women". Rumour has it that Miss Alcott has a relative now living in London who is currently working on her own autobiography, "Little Braincells".

WILLIAM THE CONQUEROR 1027-1087

L'homme qui invaded la Grande Bretagne sans cross-channel ferry ou Chunnel, et qui avez introduced notre King Harold aux archers qui étaient even encore painful que les Archers sur le radio. Tout this est chronicled dans le maintenant famous Bayeux Tapestry, que vous can voir ici.

Our Gracious Queen

"It's Anne . . . she's broken her leg."

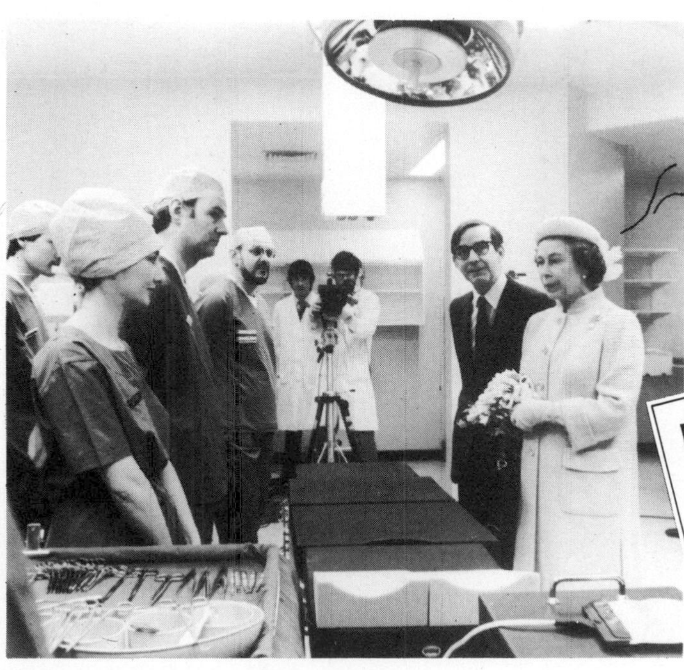

"Yes, we know about the nose job, but what have you done to Charles' little Willy?"

- The Queen is rumoured to take Harrods' sausages on every trip abroad. What or who are Andy's favourite bangers?
- True or False: Queen Diana's Honours list will include Viscount Le Bon, Lord George Michael and Dame Wayne Sleep.
- Why is Her Majesty's blotting paper always black? a) To keep all her letters secret? b) Because she can't spell?
- What evidence do you have for believing that most of the royal family are educationally sub-normal? (Try and restrict your answers to less than ten thousand words.)

"I've never said Britain is divided."
— PRINCE CHARLES quoted in The Sun.
Can he really be that short-sighted?

To commemorate the Marriage of the Prince of Wales and Lady Diana Spencer, two mugs

"I believe it won't be long before we have our first millionaire!"
— PRINCE CHARLES quoted in the Sunday Mirror.
Was he referring to the Prince of Wales' Trust or one of his relatives living off the state?

What do you give the family that has everything?

This is not The President of the United States and Mrs Reagan, as described; it is a glass bowl

One gift the royal family could not accept was a piece of cloth spun by Mr Gandhi. Apparently the royals took it as an insult, assuming it to be a loin-cloth. Rumour has it they retaliated by sending India a pair of Edward the Eighth's underpants.

Why did the United States once send Queen Elizabeth the gift of one and a half tons of nappies? Was it a) because Prince Charles had just been born? b) Because Charles announced that he was heavily into roughage? c) Because Prince Philip had started wearing bicycle clips everywhere?

Scarecrows specially designed to scare away people with brains

"My favourite programme is 'Mrs Dale's Diary'. I try never to miss it because it is the only way of knowing what goes on in a middle-class family."

— THE QUEEN MOTHER quoted in "The Royal Book of Lists"

Tom Brawn's Schooldays

Gordonstoun School
REPORT

CULLODEN TERM

NAME: Charles Philip Arthur George Windsor.

CLASS: Upper.

OVERALL DEVELOPMENT:

Poor show. The lad's turning into a lily-livered sop. What the hell's he think he's doing going supporting pansy pop-singers and Third World Aid. Doesn't he realize this conflicts with the Officer Training Corps gun-running exercises? He could do with a good stiff spell in solitary. If he wants to be head boy like his father, he better start bucking his ideas up. It's high time we started knocking some sense out of him.

A. Achilles-Rommel-Smith

Oberleutnant Adolf Achilles-Rommel-Smith

SUBJECT	GRADE	COMMENT
GLADIATING	E5	The poof put a rubber bung on the end of his spear!
VIVISECTION	Ungraded	Any more calls to Animal Rights and we'll have him flogged. Mind you, who'd want to buy him?
CHARIOT-RACING	None	One more refusal to stab the Christians at half-time and we'll put him in detention. For 4 years.
WOODWORK	E5	Pathetic! Can't even make a glider out of used matchsticks. His wooden horse wouldn't even hold three ants.

Gordonstoun Wally Club

SCHOOL NEWS

* Next term is Entebbe Term, when we shall be looking forward to armed raids on local state schools. Pupils are reminded that School Prefects may now launch Trident missiles from the school pool.

* The School Play - "Spartacus". School bully is still looking for new-born babes to be left out on the hillsides for Act One.

NOTICE TO NEW BOYS

* The day will begin with cold showers at dawn, a brisk thirty mile run and a breakfast of iced gruel.

* Any boys bringing books into school will be severely reprimanded. This is still a shooting offence.

* Following the atrocious behaviour at last end of term pillage on the local girls' school, several new boys have been made prefects.

REPORTED MISSING

* Sergeant-Major's signed copy of "Mein Kampf".

* Two lab assistants. Five-C's bomb squad are helping police with their enquiries.

NEW SCHOOL RULES

* Any boy failing to have a hairy-chest by the third year will be hung, drawn and quartered.

* There is no longer a closed season for Peasant-shooting.

* Boys must refrain from leaving nuclear waste in the quad. This should be stored in school trunks along with your grenades.

THE SCHOOL SONG

"Blades on the feuhrer"

THE SCHOOL MOTTO

Exit gender

"If only I could squeeze into tight denims and sing..."

— PRINCE CHARLES, 1985

"Why DO people think one's such a square? I mean, I tune into my fave disc jockey, Simon Dee, quite regularly. I listen to "Juke Box Jury" whenever I can. I've even sneaked under the bedcovers to tune into the Light Programme after bedtime. And I've got all sorts of discs ... The Trems, The Shads and I really think The Dave Clark Five are F.A.B.

And you can't say I'm not a hip, groovy dresser; I'm a real beatnik sometimes. I'm even getting some patterned inserts put in to turn my flares into hipster bell-bottoms.

I can't wait to take my bird to "Thunderball". Apparently 007's got an Aston just like the one the taxpayers bought me. Grooveee!"

'Wherever I lay my crown, that's my throne...'
As lead singer with The Royal Family...

'Come along
Every chap grab a gal
Everywhere, arind the realm
There'll be dancing...
Dancing in Mustique...'
as Bowie...

WINNING WAYS

Did you know that . . .

Prince Philip won the under twelves high jump medal at Cheam School with his effort of three foot ten inches? (Mind you, parents of other children complained that a man of his age should never have been allowed to enter the under twelves competition in the first place).

Lady Di won the Palmer Cup for Pets' Corner with the aid of her guinea-pig "Peanuts". (It was "Peanuts" who did the written paper).

"Peanuts" also won the Fur and Feather show at Sandringham. (The Fur and Feather show is a special competition open to all guinea-pigs owned by Di and called "Peanuts").

LOSING WAYS

Did you know that . . .

In 1977 Lady Di failed all five "O" levels twice!

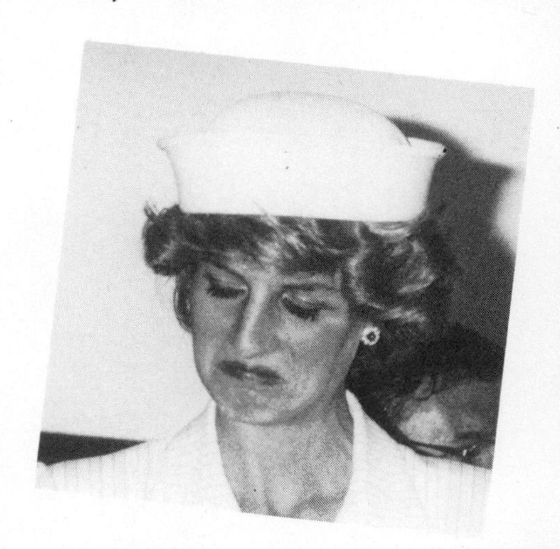

THINGS YOU CAN DO WITH LESS THAN ONE "O" LEVEL

Marry a prince

Earn a bloody fortune

Have your hair done more than once a day

Travel the world, meet interesting people and then patronize them

Appear in more Emanuels than Sylvia Kristel

Become one of Britain's leading ambassadors

Become queen

101 Uses for a dead corgi

FAVOURITE NAMES FOR PRINCES AND PRINCESSES

ANDREW

Where human bodies are ruled by messages from the brain, the bodies of Andrews, who have no brain, are governed by something much lower. The highest thing they ever concentrate on is their navel base.

Nevertheless Andies, Randies and Dandies know just how to guarantee nights in shining amour. This could explain why typical Andies spend most of their days wandering round with inane grins that hardly ever seem to go away. Andies can spend whole working days with their heads in the clouds, hovering about like something that preys on young birds.

Intellectually, history's most famous Andy was Andy Pandy.

Whenever they go walkabout in public, Elizabeth and
Philip cunningly hide themselves behind oil paintings . . .

Vol 1 No 1
CHAS
ONLY £18
We go
Queen Mum Crazy!
Charles meets the dossers — an interview with his father
VOGUE, COSMO, ELLE
Di discusses contemporary women's issues PAGE 3
WEALTH WATCHERS:
Find out how losing those excess pounds can take a weight off your mind PAGE 9
FERGUSON:
Why does she remind us of a tractor? Is she best in the field?
PAGE 142
Exclusive! Royal's secret DALLAS lovenest
BECOME QUEEN OVERNIGHT
IN OUR AMAZING DRAW!
Open to all rulers of the UK. Just send a postcard with a stamp bearing your portrait
WIN

FAVOURITE NAMES FOR PRINCES AND PRINCESSES

MARGARET

Frequently used as a popular description of a female dog, Margarets can be frightfully theatrical. Indeed they are often trying to make out that they are somebody they are not, in much the same way as the central character of the play, "Charlie's Aunt." At worst, Margarets, or Maggies, can pretend to be men, taking up jobs such as a thatcher, as a sure way of positioning themselves at the top of the house. As lovers, there's no such thing as "Maggie May"; she most certainly will, and probably already has. MARGUERITAS are drunk even more than MARGARETS. Saint Margaret is the patron saint of man-eaters.

SPIKE SAYS "CROWN HIM"

In a recent newspaper article, the famous comedian Spike Milligan, said that he would like the Queen to step down and let Prince Charles take over as monarch.

Mr Milligan also said, *"Ying tong ying tong ying tong ying tong ying tong diddle eye-po."*

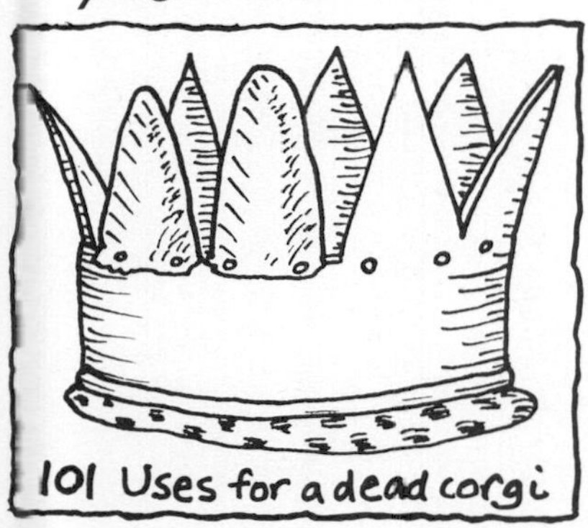

101 Uses for a dead corgi

"You won't catch me waiting for hubbie to get in before things get mended", says Royal Housewife Diana. ***"Whatever needs doing, I go right ahead and tell the staff myself."***

If you are a housewife earning over £200,000 a year, with a staff of at least 40, why not send for some of these super new DI-Y titles:

DI-Y PLUMBING

A complete course in teaching yourself how to telephone a plumber

DI-Y COMPLETE HANDYMA'AM

Step-by-step instructions on plumbing, bricklaying and roofing people's commands, including a comprehensive "*pull-ite*" guide to making a cup of tea the working class will enjoy

DI-Y DRESSMAKING

Includes the numbers of all the people who can make a dress for under £40,000

DI-Y LEAR-JET SERVICING

For Princess Anne, charity certainly begins at home, particularly work with the dumb. Here she seems to be urging Mark to take the ice-cream out of his trousers

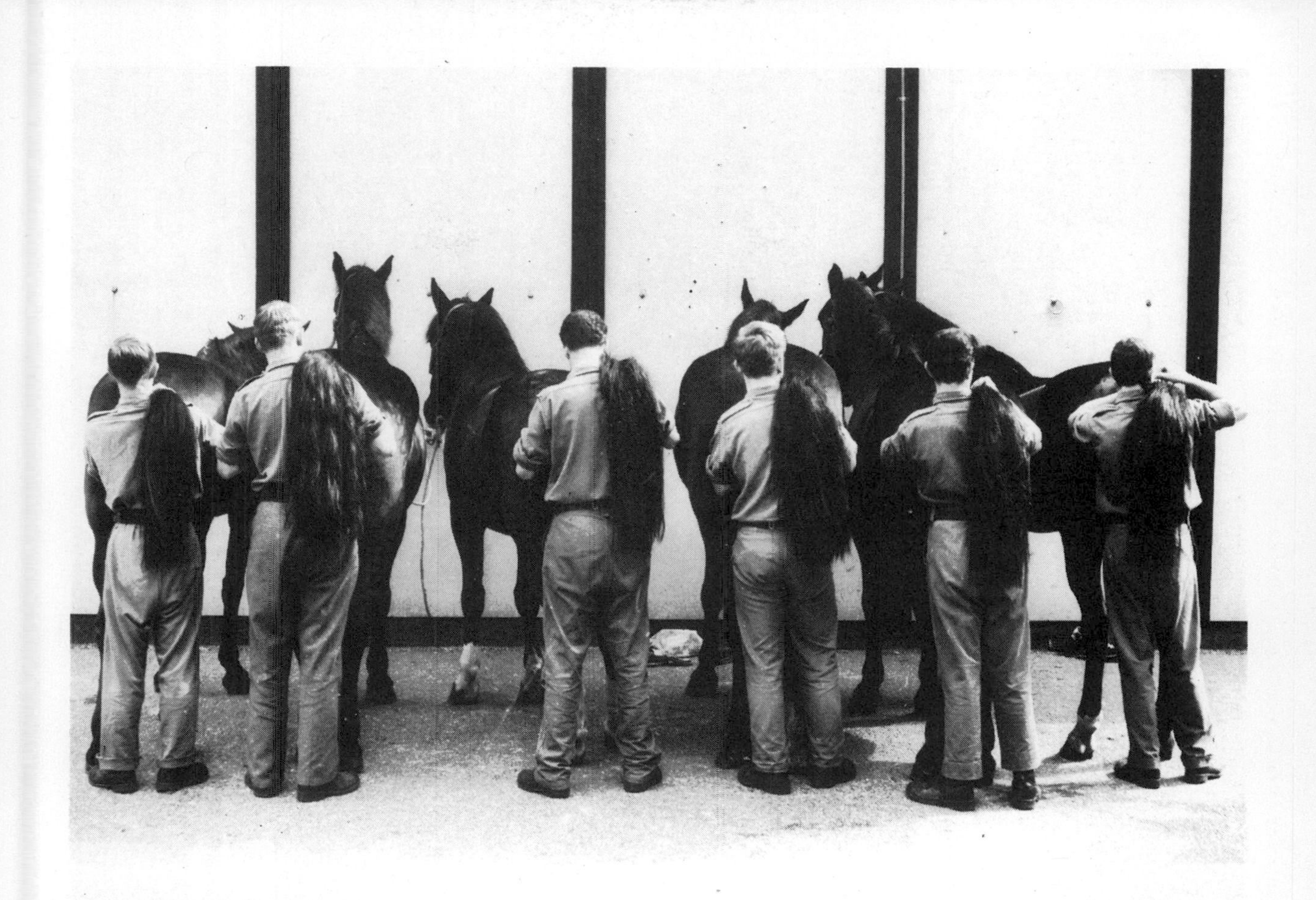

When palace security guards say they check everywhere, they mean everywhere

FAVOURITE NAMES FOR PRINCES AND PRINCESSES

DIANA

From the Welsh "Di" or "Dye", meaning "artificial hair colourant" or simply "artificial". Even today, Dianas still try to turn themselves into something they are not. In much the same way as Cinderella, seeing her elder, ugly sister with a prince, transformed herself into Diana the Huntress, using everything from Fairy Godmothers to magic pumpkins to fanatical diets and nose jobs to try and outshine her. Mind you, Dianas are considerably less bright than their glittering clothes may suggest. At school, Dianas wear hats with their initial on.

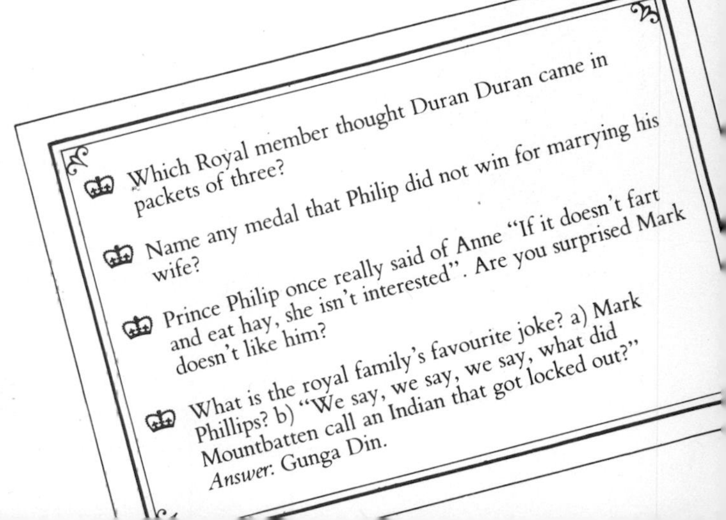

- Which Royal member thought Duran Duran came in packets of three?
- Name any medal that Philip did not win for marrying his wife?
- Prince Philip once really said of Anne "If it doesn't fart and eat hay, she isn't interested". Are you surprised Mark doesn't like him?
- What is the royal family's favourite joke? a) Mark Phillips? b) "We say, we say, we say, what did Mountbatten call an Indian that got locked out?" *Answer*: Gunga Din.

a is for aristocrats
b is for barbour
e is for emanuels
f is fake corgi biggies
"Chuls, when you were a baby, what did your mummy give you to keep you quiet?"
"This little piggy went to Harrods . . ."
"Cornwall"
z is for zandra rhodes
w is for walk-man
x is what Koo's films are
v is for vidal basoon
y is everybody else so poor?
u are an overprivileged wally
t is what plebs have instead of supper

g is fo[r] gucci h is for hooray C is for the county Wills will take over from Daddy I is for Ingland

Royal mum Diana discusses what it's like to be a royal mum called Diana . . .

"Cripes! I thought, when Chuls first told me I was preggers. I'd been wondering what the lump was. Gosh, help, panic and all that! Fancy me having a bun in the Aga!"

"Actually being a royal mum's actually triff, actually. For a start you simply can't get woken by a baby that's crying forty rooms away. And even if they do cry, if a royal baby needs a dummy, you just send for its father. Giggle, giggle. Tee hee, what a wheeze."

"I remember Chuls asking me if I'd consider breast-feeding. Perhaps I'd been holding my knife and fork wrongly . . . tee-hee . . . Oh, and giving birth . . . before I had Wills the only labour pain I'd encountered was Arthur Scargill . . . hee-hee-hee . . ."

Mothers' questions answered

Q: What should a royal mum do if a royal baby wakes at night?
A: Sack nanny

Q: Can being surrounded by upper-class nerds stunt a child's growth?
A: Only mentally, and this will never affect job prospects anyway

Q: Do royal babies suck their thumbs?
A: Of course not, there are staff to do that for them

Q: Who painted all those lovely little pictures in the royal doll's house?
A: Van Dyck

The Queen of Hearts
She made some tarts
And so did Uncle Andy

HOMEWORK FOR WILLIAM

Write a short story on the subject "Imagine what it would be like not to be a prince for a day".
Please ask whoever writes this for you to write illegibly so we can give you the benefit of the doubt.

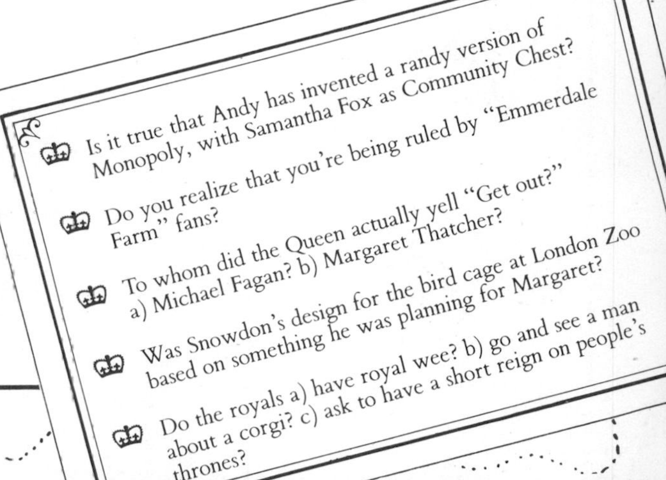
Is it true that Andy has invented a randy version of Monopoly, with Samantha Fox as Community Chest?

Do you realize that you're being ruled by "Emmerdale Farm" fans?

To whom did the Queen actually yell "Get out?" a) Michael Fagan? b) Margaret Thatcher?

Was Snowdon's design for the bird cage at London Zoo based on something he was planning for Margaret?

Do the royals a) have royal wee? b) go and see a man about a corgi? c) ask to have a short reign on people's thrones?

n is for nina ricci O is for OK Yar! K is for kavia[r] J is for jumped up prat

m is for masons where uncle gets stoned q is something we'll never have to do

MONARCHY PLC

First British Telecom, then British Gas, and now...

THE ROYAL BUSINESS GOES PUBLIC!

Yes, this is your chance to buy shares in ***THE FIRM***

* **Every shareholder receives:**
An individual vote of future hairstyles and dresses. The chance to choose your own three words in the Christmas speech. Princess Michael to open the motorway service area of your choice.

* **MAJOR shareholders receive:**
A special time-share apartment in the palace of their own choice. **PLUS** — Their very own name on the Corgi walking rota. Special discounts on coins and stamps showing the company chairman.

NOW
is the time to
INVEST
in your own
INVESTITURE!

Men, you can be called "Sir" for two weeks a year!
Ladies, you can be called "Ladies"!
For more details of Time-share Knighthoods and other titles, write to Monarchy PLC, The Mall.

ASSETS INCLUDE:

International diplomatic twit, Philip estimated value £1.50

Future chairman Charles - estimated value £20

International celebrity Diana - estimated value £350 million

The richest woman in the world, "E.R." - estimated value £6000 million

FURTHER ASSETS INCLUDE:
The rich man's Liz Taylor, endless personalised stamps and coins, one army, one navy, one air force, one government, Olympic showjumpers and any pink bits you can still see on the map.

YOUR NAME GOES HERE

Yes, Monarchy Promotions can get your name or your company message seen in all the highest places. With fantastic TV coverage.

Turn Sovereigns into Gold!

As part of Monarchs Incorporated you're allowed a complete monopoly! You pay no tax! No 'phone-bills! You can't be sued! You never have to give a toss about politics! There's no union! No strikes!

With proper merchandising of weddings, scandals and endorsements, you could have a stake in the biggest money-making machine since the royal mint. (Buy enough shares and you'll even get a go on that too!)

New! Yes, major shareholders in The Firm can now get a 100th Birthday telegram years ahead of non-shareholders!

ROYALWORLD

The most privileged place on earth!

Fabulous Fun for ALL the family!

PAY ONE PRICE* and stay all day!!

* just £1 million

Yes ***Real Royals*** are waiting to greet you at

ROYALWORLD

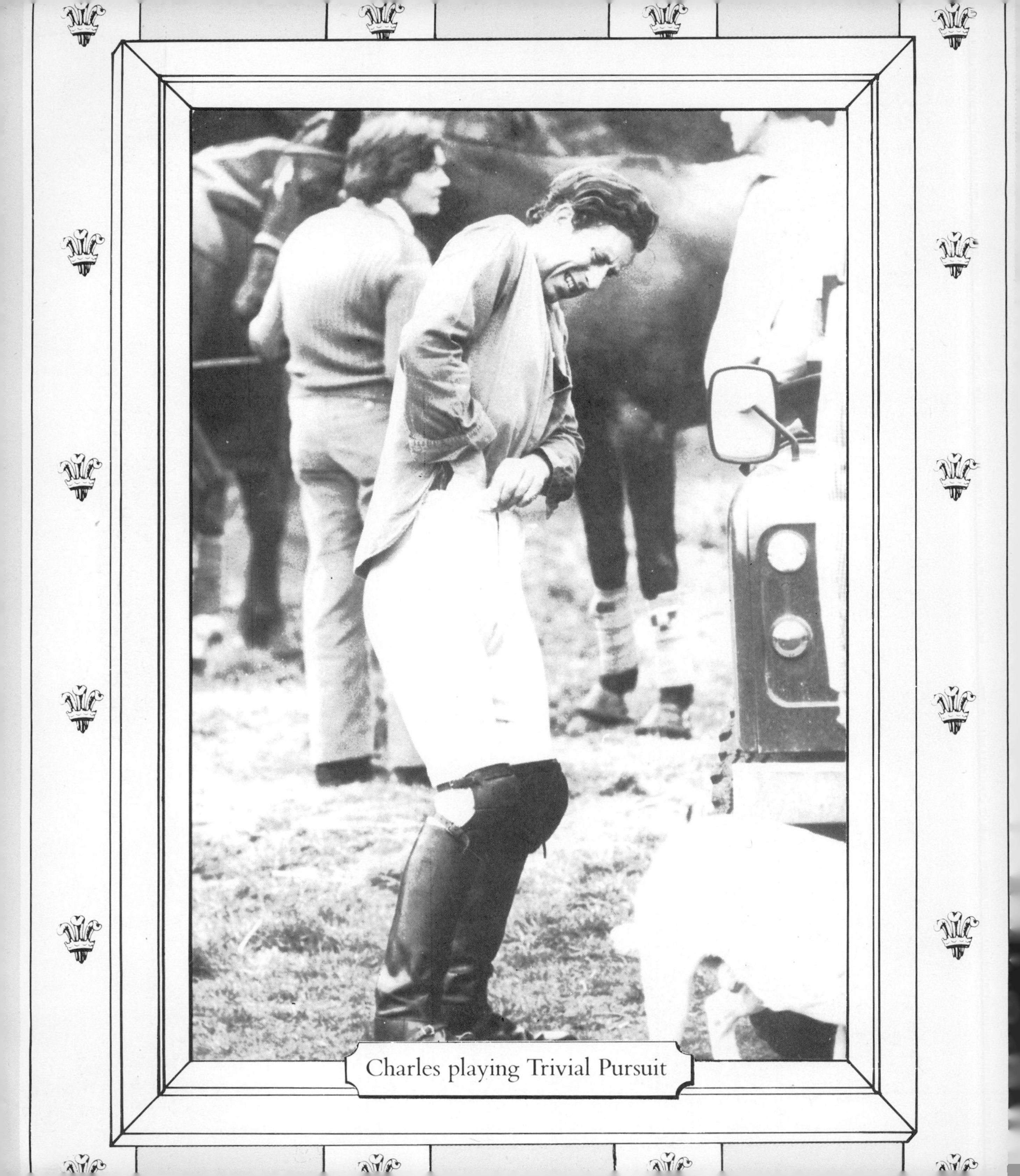

Charles playing Trivial Pursuit

Andy practises for a long spell at sea

How to save Britain millions

The Queen's Christmas message to the author

ABOUT THE AUTHOR
Tim John has written for Central Television's "Spitting Image", Channel 4's "The Max Headroom Show" and Radio 4's "Weekending". He was not educated at Gordonstoun and Sandhurst. Nor were most of the people who went there. Had he had a different surname, the British taxpaying public would have given him £20,000 a year for going to University, plus a free country estate for marrying his wife.

Following the publication of this book, Tim is currently working on his escape from the Tower of London.

With Special Thanks To:

Jo and Eleanor for all their support, to Sue and Christy for their inspired designs, to Rob Shreeve for taking the royal family on, to Colin Murray and Mark Lucas for keeping the battle going, to Nick Webb for forsaking any hope of ever receiving a knighthood and to Liz, Phil, Chuls, Di, Randy, Fergie, Queen Victoria, Henry VIII, and all the other Throne Rangers without whom none of this would have been possible.

PICTURE CREDITS
Alpha, BBC Hulton Picture Library, Camera Press Ltd, CPNA Pool, Mary Evans Picture Library, Fox Keystone, Popperfoto, Rex Features Ltd, Paul Rider, Garbor Scott, Syndication International